The Entrepr Visionary

The Dynamics of Entrepreneurial Leadership

Andre Thomas

GREATNESS
PUBLISHING

www.ideasandsolutions.org

Cover Design and Formatting by Farouk J. Roberts
Brands & Love Creative
www.brandsnlove.com

Library and Archives Canada
ISBN: 978-1-927579-07-7

Dedication

This book is dedicated to
The Ideas and Solutions Group Inc. team.

We are destined to bring change to our world
as we work together in synergy.

Acknowledgements

A special thanks to my wife,
Nina D. Thomas for typing out this manuscript.

Thanks to Farouk J. Roberts for
the cover design and formatting.

Thanks to Valentine Dantes for your editing.

Contents

The Entrepreneurial Gift

1~
Natural-Born Entrepreneurs

An entrepreneur is a person who creates goods and services that add value to people at a profit.

True entrepreneurs are indispensable to the economies of nations. The gift in them creates goods and services that add value to people at a profit. Their enterprises create hundreds of millions of jobs on the earth. When you find a society in which entrepreneurial ideas and the way of the entrepreneur is not embraced and celebrated, systemic poverty is always present. Entrepreneurs come in different shapes, ages, ethnic groups, gender and education. However, the gift in them is uniform. It is a gift that sees opportunities in the market place and creates products that would meet the needs of people in exchange for financial profit.

In my study of entrepreneurs over the years, I have come to realize that they come in four categories.

1. Self-Employed Entrepreneurs – these are entrepreneurs whose goods and services create employment for only themselves.

2. The Single Business Entrepreneur – these are gifted to create a small business that can grow and become a medium or large size company.

3. The Serial Entrepreneurial – these are gifted to create multiple businesses ranging from two to as many as one hundred, depending on their leadership gifting, ability and passion.

4. The Investor Entrepreneur – these have money to invest and are gifted in creating profits by buying a stake in other people's businesses.

ARE YOU AN ENTREPRENEUR?

Whilst entrepreneurship can be studied, researched and taught, the gift of the entrepreneur is genetic. It is no different from the genetic gift to be an opera singer, you either have it or you don't. There are certain characteristics that come with the genetic gift of the entrepreneur which we will now explore. However, I must first define what a genetic gift is:

A genetic gift is an innate skill, ability or talent that a person possesses which enables him or her to perform a significant task with the minimum amount of time, effort and learning.

A Glimpse of Entrepreneurship in 7 Year Olds

I experienced this once when my daughter Simone and her friend Sesime spent a day at the beautiful Mullins beach in Barbados. They were both about seven years old and came back from their day long adventure with Barbados twenty-two dollars and fifty cents in a jar. Sesime's father and I were in shock when our children proceeded to joyfully tell us that they had money. With unrehearsed synchronization and a bit of Gestapo tactics, we immediately, proceeded to question them on how they acquired that money, since they didn't get it from us. The children nonchalantly and gleefully informed us that while they were at the beach, they saw scores of tourists and sun lovers enjoying themselves and thought they were the perfect targets to make extra money. When we heard that, the pitch in our questions was raised another decibel. Then in their nonchalant style they went on to explain that they saw some rocks on the beach and decided to pick them up, clean them and sell them to the tourists and sun lovers as souvenirs and paper weights. Our mouths fell open. What was even more amazing was that these two seven year olds were able to sell twenty-two dollars and fifty cents worth of stones. Our anxiety quickly turned into celebration as we came to the realization that we had two natural-born entrepreneurs for children.

This is the purity of the gift. The ability to take what others see as common, add your special touch to it and then sell it to others who enjoy its new heightened value at a profit.

There are several characteristics that come with the genetic gift of an entrepreneur even when it's displayed in a child.

1. Vision

It is a clear mental portrait of a future that can be possessed. One of the defining traits of entrepreneurship is the ability to spot an opportunity and imagine something where others haven't. Entrepreneurs have an innate curiosity that identifies overlooked niches and puts them at the forefront of innovation. They see another world and have the ability to communicate that vision effectively to partners, investors, customers and staff.

On a scale of one to ten with one being the least and ten being the highest, what is your level of strength in spotting opportunities and casting a compelling vision about it?

1	2	3	4	5	6	7	8	9	10

2. Innovation

It is thinking outside the box of history to create new ways to solve old problems. It is the hallmark of all entrepreneurs who bring new services, products, goods, systems and experiences to the world.

On a scale of one to ten with one being the least and ten being the highest, state your level of strength in innovation.

1	2	3	4	5	6	7	8	9	10

3. Persuasiveness

The ability to sell your ideas, opinions, products and services is a distinguishing mark of all entrepreneurs. They are persuasive people and as the saying goes, they can sell ice to an Eskimo, once they believe in it. The difference between a person with a genetic gift to sell and an entrepreneur is that an entrepreneur is persuasive about products they are passionate about. A classic sales person can sell any product even if they don't believe in it.

On a scale of one to ten with one being the least and ten being the highest, what is your level of strength in selling a product you believe in?

1	2	3	4	5	6	7	8	9	10

4. Passion

Passion is desire at boiling point. When desire is at boiling point it moves people into action. True entrepreneurs are action-orientated and are not commentators or focused only on research. While others may comment about what they do, the boiling desires in entrepreneurs compels them to take risks and invest to create new products for humanity to enjoy.

On a scale of one to ten with one being the least and ten being the highest, what is your level of passion in taking a product that you believe in to the market place?

1	2	3	4	5	6	7	8	9	10

5. Tenacity

Starting and running a business is not a sprint; it's a marathon. You have to be able to live with uncertainty and hurdle over many obstacles for years on end as you pursue your entrepreneurial dream. You have to outlast your mistakes and not surrender to your competition and produce consistent quality to your customers even when the immediate future is ambiguous.

On a scale of one to ten with one being the least and ten being the highest, what is your level of entrepreneurial tenacity?

1	2	3	4	5	6	7	8	9	10

6. Proactive

A proactive person takes responsibility to do what is required to create the future they desire. True entrepreneurs take responsibility to do all that is required to create and sell their products.

On a scale of one to ten with one being the least and ten being the highest, what is your level of proactivity in business?

1	2	3	4	5	6	7	8	9	10

7. Tolerance of Ambiguity and Risk

This is the ability to rise above the fear of uncertainty and potential failure and still deliver your product. It empowers a person to live with risks without being a nervous wreck. It is an indispensable trait of all entrepreneurs.

On a scale of one to ten with one being the least and ten being the highest, what is your level of tolerance, ambiguity and risk?

1	2	3	4	5	6	7	8	9	10

8. Flexibility

The ability to adapt your product, systems and operations to suit a market is a hallmark of successful entrepreneurs. For many entrepreneurs, their final product when it enters the market does not exactly look like the product when it was first conceptualized.

On a scale of one to ten with one being the least and ten being the highest, what is your level of flexibility to adapt a product to suit a market?

1	2	3	4	5	6	7	8	9	10

9. Self Confidence

Confidence is the ability to boldly express your ideas, opinions and products to others. True confidence is the opposite of arrogance. Confidence is an authentic expression whilst arrogance is a veneer. Self-confidence is magnetic whilst arrogance repels.

On a scale of one to ten with one being the least and ten being the highest, what is your level of self-confidence?

1	2	3	4	5	6	7	8	9	10

10. Tradition-breaking

Entrepreneurs are more passionate about what can be than what is. They are creatures of innovation and not servants of tradition. They break the rules of tradition in their quests to bring new products into the marketplace. The fact that it has never been done before doesn't scare but actually excites them.

On a scale of one to ten with one being the least and ten being the highest, what is your level of tradition-breaking in your entrepreneurial pursuits?

1	2	3	4	5	6	7	8	9	10

11. Market Awareness

A true entrepreneur innately scans the market place and assesses needs and gaps. It is this trait of their gift that empowers them to create goods and services that gain traction in the marketplace.

On a scale of one to ten with one being the least and ten being the highest, what is your level of marketplace awareness?

1	2	3	4	5	6	7	8	9	10

12. Entrepreneurial Networking

True entrepreneurs are gifted in building networks of investors, partners, customers and staff in order to see their entrepreneurial visions come to pass. People are the wheels of any enterprise and mature entrepreneurs have learnt how to work with people and through people to accomplish their uncommon dreams.

On a scale of one to ten with one being the least and ten being the highest, state your level of entrepreneurial networking.

1	2	3	4	5	6	7	8	9	10

YOUR ENTREPRENEURIAL SCORE CARD

Draw a circle around the number that best describes the strength of the various attributes of your entrepreneurial gift. It is important that you are totally honest with yourself and if you need another opinion, ask someone close to you, who will tell you the truth no matter what.

To find your average score, which will reveal the strength of your entrepreneurial gift, add your score in each of the twelve categories and divide by twelve.

Your highest possible score will be 10, which is 120 divided by 10. A person with a strong entrepreneurial gift will have an average score between 7 and 10. A person with a medium entrepreneurial gift will score an average of 6.

What is your score?

If your score is 6 and above you have an entrepreneurial gift.

What type of entrepreneur are you?

1. Self-Employed Entrepreneur

2. Single Business Entrepreneur

3. The Serial Entrepreneur ☐

4. The Investor Entrepreneur ☐

The Products

2 ~
Defining Your Products

An entrepreneur without a product is like a chef without a kitchen

The process of the entrepreneur or product development team choosing the products that the company will take to the marketplace is arguably one of the most important processes in entrepreneurialism. This process is further complicated by the fact that the market for entrepreneurial products is not static, but moving. A product that is relevant in a segment of the market can become irrelevant six months later. I have likened choosing your product as an entrepreneur to the skill of pigeon shooting.

Those who pigeon shoot know that you aim your riffle at the immediate flight of the pigeon. This is because by the time your bullet gets to where the pigeon was inflight when you saw it, it would have left. This is because the pigeon is in motion and not static. All markets are in motion. What does a skillful pigeon shooter do? He shoots at the immediate trajectory of the pigeon, which is just in front of it so that the pigeon and the bullet could have a rendezvous in the air. This is the art of finding your product and bringing it to the market.

Let's look at the example of Blockbuster LLC.

From Market Leader to Bankruptcy

Blockbuster LLC formerly Blockbuster Entertainment Inc. was an American base provider of home movies and video games rental services. It grew through video rental shops both owned and franchised. Later adding DVD by mail, streaming, video on demand and Cinema Theater. At its peak in 2004, blockbuster had up to sixty thousand employees and more than nine thousand stores.

However, the story changed due to the fact that markets do not remain static, and are perpetually in motion driven by forces that entrepreneurs cannot control. The force that brought about this change was the rise of the Internet and the increasing download speeds available to homes across America. A new company saw the opportunity called Netflix and they did not follow the tradition of opening video stores. What they did was to put all their movies on an internet portal and for a subscription fee have people download and watch their movies in the comfort of their homes without going into their cars or taking a walk to their local blockbuster video store. All customers needed to have was a credit card, and they could watch movies on their laptop, home computers or on their televisions, using external devices like Xbox.

Blockbuster failed to respond to this change in market conditions driven by Internet streaming and ended up busted. Blockbuster lost significant revenue and filed for bankruptcy on September 23, 2010. On April 06, 2011, the company and its remaining one thousand seven hundred stores was bought by satellite television provider Dish Network at an auction price of two hundred and thirty three million and the assumption of eighty seven million in liabilities and other obligations. After the acquisition, Dish Network closed two hundred branches in July 2011, five hundred more in the first half of 2012 and another three hundred in 2013. In November 2013, it was announced that the remaining three hundred owned stores would also close, (though fifty franchise owned stores would continue to remain open). The company's DVD by mail rental service was also due to seize operations as well. As you can see, it was not a good acquisition for the Dish Network as the market was changing every quarter, thus making it increasingly difficult to create profits selling videos as before.

With the benefit of hindsight you may ask the question, why did Blockbuster not see this coming and enter into the streaming video market? You may also ask why did the Dish Network spend so much money trying to resurrect a dying dinosaur?

Let us now examine the common mistakes that even the most successful entrepreneurs make.

1. Passion for a new product that is not relevant to the marketplace.

Passion as I said earlier, is desire at boiling point and would always move you into action. Entrepreneurs can sometimes be deceived and blinded by their passion when they do not look at their products through the lens of the current market reality.

Let me illustrate this with a diagram I call **The Circle of Entrepreneurial Deception**.

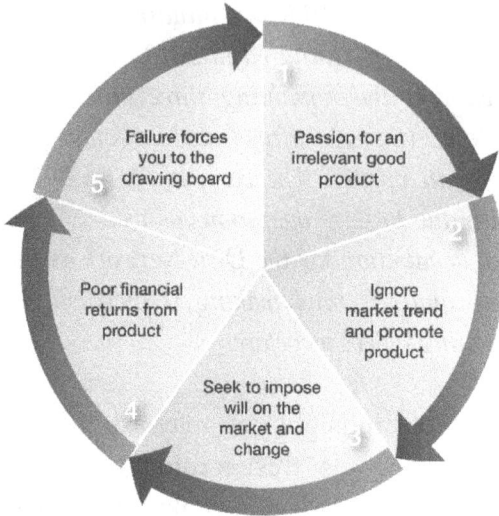

2. Passion for a product with a successful history that is fast losing its relevance in an evolving marketplace.

The story of Blockbuster illustrates this mistake. In its boom years, it generated hundreds of millions in profits. However, its obsession with the business model that created the millions of dollars in profit caused it to be unresponsive to the changing home movie marketplace. Entrepreneurs must never become obsessed with a successful business model. This is because, *success is a perishable asset.* Blockbuster success perished.

3. Bringing New Products To The Market

In bringing new products to the market, there are four major things that must be considered in your product development process.

1. Can the product become first, second or third in its market?

2. Do you and your team have passion for the product?

3. Does the product create a financial engine?

4. Do you and your team have or can acquire the know-how to deliver the product with excellence?

A Product Launch Nightmare: The story of the HP Touch Pad Tablet

The HP Touch Pad is a Tablet computer which was developed and designed by Hewlett-Packard. It was launched July 01, 2011 in the United States and subsequently in Canada, United Kingdom, Germany and Australia. Early reviews of the HP Touch Pad were mixed. David Pouge of the New York times wrote, "It works beautifully and conveys far more information than the iPad 2." This tablet was designed to be an iPad beater. However, on August 18, 2012, forty nine days after the touchpad was launched in the

United States, Hewlett-Packered announced that it would be discontinuing all current hardware devices running webOS.

Remaining touchpad stock received substantial price reductions and quickly sold out.

HP, a company with a billion dollar revenue had made a classic mistake. They allowed their passion to produce an iPad killer tablet to blind them to the fact that no tablet without the Android or Apple operating system was going to excel. This was a market reality as the Android operating system offered customers a multiple choice of phones and the Apple tablet appealed to those who wanted an iconic brand.

The spectacular failure of this new product launch was due to its strategic decision to run its HP Touch Pad on an HP developed operating system. This was doomed to fail as they could not compete with the access to applications that Apple and Android users had.

The Strategic Product Development Wisdom of The Amazon Kindle

Amazon on the other hand, when they decided to create a tablet called Kindle Fire decided to use a custom designed Android operating system. Customers began receiving their Kindle Fires on November 15, 2011 and by the following December, customers had purchased over a million Kindle devices per week. International data corporation IDC estimated that the Kindle Fire sold about 4.7 million units during the fourth quarter of 2011. As of May 2013 about 7 million units were sold according to estimates, which has now placed it as the number two best-selling tablet after Apple's iPad.

Think about it, Amazon is not a computer manufacturing company; its core business is the selling of books and other merchandise online. HP on the other hand, is one of the world's largest computer manufacturing companies and yet Amazon had greater strategic wisdom than HP in the tablet market. While the Touch Pad with its irrelevant webOS operating system was being discontinued, Amazon was in the same period on the fast track to sell 4.7 million units. This is the power of strategic wisdom in product development.

STOP AND REFLECT

Evaluating the Viability of Existing Products.
I will now list several questions that I will ask as a strategy consultant to businesses. Use them the to help you evaluate the relevance of your product inventory.

1.   What is the position of the product in the marketplace at the moment; is it falling, rising or maintaining its position?

2.   What are the trends in the market and what do they indicate about the viability of the product in its current condition?

3.   Are there new significant players coming into the market with innovative approaches that may cause you to lose market share?

4.   Are you willing to change a current business model that is about to take a nosedive if required?

3~

The DNA Of A Great Product Delivery Model

A great product solves a problem for enough people in a marketplace at a price that's affordable to create profit

Deoxyribonucleic acid (DNA) is a molecule that encodes the genetic instructions used in the development and functioning of all known living organisms and many viruses. All great product delivery models have essentially the same DNA.

1. A great product solves a problem for a person

Business is simply about creating products that solve problems for people. It also involves convincing them that your product would best solve their problem and delivering the product at a price that creates profit for you and is affordable for them. If your product does not solve a problem, you are out of business. You may also have a product that used to solve a problem for multitudes of people, but because of market trends that number is significantly reducing. This would have been the case for the makers of the Walkman. The Walkman was a device that allowed you to put a cassette in a mobile tape deck and listen to music through earphones on the move. I watched as shelves in stores began to change as new devices like the iPod and other digital musical devices started to make the Walkman look like a dinosaur. These devices were able to carry sometimes more than a thousand songs, whereas the Walkman or mobile CD player could only play a limited amount. They both solved the same problem, which was create musical pleasure on the move for the user. However, the digital music recorder like the iPod quickly became the product to have as it offers so much more.

2. A great product is priced at a level its market can afford

A good product with no sales is headed for the scrapyard. Knowing what your market can afford and developing and pricing your product with that in mind, is crucial. Immature entrepreneurs many times price a product based on how much money they need at that time and not at what the market can afford so they sabotage their business. A wise entrepreneur in his pricing determines whether he is going for volume or smaller high financial value sales.

3. A great product delivery model makes the product easily accessible to its potential customers

Access is a big word in business, and depending on your nature of business your level of access would significantly impact your success or failure. If you operate a retail outlet and customers cannot find your shop, you are in trouble. If you operate a consultant business and customers cannot view your services on the Internet or call you on the phone, you are in trouble. In other words, giving the potential end user of your product easy access to the product is imperative.

4. A great product delivery model is operated by passionate informed sales people

Informed passionate people selling products are indispensable. I have walked into many stores where the sales staff acted like they were doing me a favor when I wanted to find out about their products. I would often wonder to myself whether or not these persons were aware that they were actually sabotaging the business. There are also times when staff does not know enough about what they are selling and this doesn't inspire confidence in the buyer. A wise entrepreneur ensures that his or her sales staff has a healthy balance of passion and product knowledge.

5. A great product delivery model is responsive to customer product needs

A great product delivery model finds a way to systemize the reporting of the client product needs back to the product development department.

6. A great product delivery model is responsive to problems with the product

When the product is faulty the response of customer service is critical. In this world where opinions can go around the world via social media, cellphones and YouTube, keeping your customer happy is important. One passionate, determined, informed and unhappy customer can cause a lot of damage. So it is important to have a good problem solving policy that does not punish your customers for buying faulty goods from you.

7. A great product delivery model is customer service driven

Great entrepreneurs know that the customer is king. That's the secret of Wal-Mart, one of the greatest businesses in our day. The satisfaction of your customer is one of your greatest guarantees in business.

8. A great product delivery model is culturally intelligent

Product delivery is not only a science; it's an art form. Culturally intelligent entrepreneurs understand this very well and adapt their product offerings to make them appealing to the people group they are attempting to reach. An example of this, is that at one time Kentucky Fried Chicken in Barbados had a fish sandwich on its menu whilst the KFC in Highpoint North Carolina had a Sunday buffet that came with chicken livers. Wise entrepreneurs add small features to their core products to make them appealing to different people groups within their market.

9. A great product delivery model is not cast in stone but responsive to market trends

Flexibility to market trends is a hallmark for entrepreneurs who have developed their innovative attributes. They seek to stay in sync with the trajectory of the market. This is applicable to a small food vendor who is self-employed or to a large multi-National Company like Apple computers. I have seen small food vendors create a diet menu to appeal to an overweight population seeking to lose weight.

This is no different than the wisdom of Apple computers creating the IPhone and designing it with the capability of a five star phone, digital music capacity of the IPod and the camera quality of a standard digital camera. They created a device that made millions of people dump their cell phone and their economy digital camera.

Flexibility and innovation is seen in the evolution that took the IPod and turned it into an IPhone, which then evolved into another product called the IPad Tablet.

10. A great product delivery model has an early warning system

When you study the demise of companies like Blockbuster and Chrysler, you realize that they did not have an effective early warning executive decision making system. In

Chrysler's case they continued manufacturing cars using the same business model in spite of the meteoric rise of the Japanese and Korean car manufactures in the USA. They only dealt with the poor business model when the business filed for bankruptcy. They could have changed the model before if their passion to stay in business was greater than the pain the process would have caused.

Here are some strategic questions that I encourage you to stop, reflect, and discuss with your team.

What are the problems that your core products are designed to solve?

_____

_____

_____

_____

_____

_____

_____

What are the solutions that your products offer?

_____

_____

_____

_____

_____

_____

_____

Are there any existing competitors offering better solutions than you?

_____

_____

_____

_____

_____

_____

Are there any emerging companies that could affect your market share?

_____

_____

_____

_____

_____

_____

Define the existing markets for your product?

_____

_____

_____

_____

_____

_____

_____

The world is now a global village. Are there new markets beyond your local jurisdiction that will be attracted to the solutions your products provide?

_____

_____

_____

_____

_____

_____

_____

National Entrepreneurial Culture

4~
Understanding Your Entrepreneurial Culture

Seeking to influence a territory without understanding its culture is setting the venture up for a loss

Culture can be defined as the totality of attitudes, customs and beliefs that distinguish one group of people from another. The general culture of a people group is made up of many subcultures. For the purposes of this book, we will examine the entrepreneurial subculture of nations. In my personal studies of national entrepreneurial cultures, I have identified five distinct cultures.

They are:

1.   A Systemic Poverty Culture
2.   A Crab Culture

3. A Passive Service Culture
4. A Dream Culture
5. A Commonwealth Culture

1 - A SYSTEMIC POVERTY CULTURE

As the phrase suggests, systemic poverty is generational and people within that culture do not have a wealth creating ideology. There are no informal or formal processes and systems within the culture to facilitate major entrepreneurial pursuits. The culture is built on survival and whatsoever is required to be done whether it's beg, prostitute, steal or in some cases, do micro-business to put some food on the table.

This culture tends not to be adversarial to business as long as the entity is not seen as taking advantage of the community. If they think that your business is there to exploit them, they may become hostile and in some cases, may seek to sabotage it because they don't have much to lose.,

Creating a successful business in this culture involves not only creating your own sub-culture within the company that is entrepreneurial, but also engaging in community transformation projects. This is very important as people generally in that community would support a business that they think is in their strategic interest. Examples of companies that have not followed this wisdom and have reaped a world wind of trouble would be some of the oil companies that are based in Algeria, Chad and certain parts of Nigeria. In June 2013, a group that believed that the oil company was exploiting the region killed twenty-three oil workers in a fiery assault.

In summary, great profits can be made from doing business where there is systemic poverty, because of zero competition from the local population. This is particular true when the core business involves the extraction of natural resources from the region. However, this can become a poisoned chalice if you do not meaningfully engage the community in social transformation projects in such a way that they celebrate your presence in the community. Failure to do this may leave you open to revolutionary members of the community and acts of sabotage. World trends indicate that the increased spreading of revolutionary sentiment among marginalized people groups and the proliferation of weapons will cause more uprising within disaffected communities in the next decade. In other words, create handsome profits but make sure you reinvest a portion of that back into the community to guarantee your continual safe presence in that environment.

2 - A CRAB CULTURE

Crabs are very interesting creatures and we can learn about the dynamics of certain people groups from how they operate. My first encounter with the crab culture is when I attended a fish market in the city of London, England at about 5am in the morning.

A Crab Lesson in London

I love fish and my friends had informed me that this was the best place in London to buy wholesale fish. As I went through the fish market looking at all different types of fish, I was shocked and stunned when I got to the crab section of the market.

The first thing that struck me was that all the crabs were alive and moving in this huge basket piled one on top each other. However, this large basket had no cover, so I thought to myself, "Oh my gosh, they forgot to cover it and the crabs would escape and go all over the market." As I proceeded to ask a member of staff why the baskets were not covered, he asked me to take a closer look at the baskets. This is what I saw. I saw crab after crab, attempt to escape from the basket and each time they tried, some of the other crabs nearest to that one pulled it back into the basket. The staff member then told me, "If more than two crabs are in a basket, a cover is unnecessary as each would not allow the other to escape."

There are people groups that have a crab culture. This crab culture manifests in the following ways:

1. People within the culture are very critical of new ideas, innovation and progressive visionary people.

2. Envy is bitterness of the success of others. In this culture, envy reigns and visionaries are envied for a vision they may have potential to achieve. If possible envious people take steps to sabotage that vision.

3. People within this culture prefer to imitate what progressive entrepreneurs are doing so that they can dilute their success rather than blaze a new trail for themselves.

4. People within this culture tend to have friends who like them when they are average and oppose them if they become outstanding.

5. People within this culture tend to have their greatest critics among their own siblings, extended family and fake friends who compete with them to see who will be the first to get out of the basket of mediocrity.

6. People within this culture attack those, who in the beginning of their entrepreneurial journeys make business failures. They don't encourage them when they are down, but rather take pleasure in shooting the wounded.

7. People within this culture, though successful, tend to resent when others become successful through partnership or use of their products. In their minds, only they should be successful. They have this philosophy, *"Get all you can, can all you get, sit on the can and shoot anybody who wants anything from your can."*

In the crab culture, people find satisfaction in being the only big fish in a small aquarium and work covertly to prevent others from achieving their dreams.

Starting and sustaining a successful business in this culture is possible, however great wisdom is required to take off like a rocket and stay high enough beyond the reach of the crabs.

❖ **Wisdom for building an enterprise within a crab culture**

Startup Wisdom:

✓ Qualify the trustworthiness of people before you share the details of your vision.

✓ Build layers of intimacy within your dream team.

Intimacy literally means in-to-me-see. Wise people allow people to see into them based on levels of access. In the pursuit of your vision, your team must be made up of the following people:

1. Implementation staff and partners (Lower level of intimacy)

2. Creative and strategic partners and staff (Higher level of intimacy)

3. Business Confidants (Transparency)

✓ You must communicate with all people on a *"need to know basis"*

The army uses this system, as information is a weapon. It makes sure to give soldiers only the information required to execute their assignment just in case he or she turns out to be a secret enemy. To get higher levels of information you need to get security clearance. As an entrepreneur in a crab culture environment, this approach can save your business.

❖ **Wisdom for Working with Government and Lending Agencies**

Just today my wife and I had a conversation with a talented couple that were approved for a loan by a government-lending corporation to secure a business. To their horror, the lending officer after reading their business plan, saw it was a winning business strategy and contacted another person and gave him or her access to their confidential business plan. This officer also gave the recipient of the couple's business plan the loan to carry out the plan and start the venture. This kind of sabotage is very typical in crab cultures and is done in both government and traditional lending agencies, like banks.

This is my strategic counsel when dealing with government lending agencies or banks:

✓ Create two versions of your business plans. The first plan is your Business Strategic Plan, which would include every detail that should be used in the business. The second should be an Investors Business Plan, which would be on a need to know bases and only contain the information that is required for the government agency or lending institution to make their decisions. Do not add anything more and keep some of your cards close to your chest.

❖ **Wisdom for operating with partners and customers**

✓ In this culture, except you are dealing with a proven and trusted relationship, do not enter into any business relationship without a signed contract that specifies terms, and conditions and opt out clauses.

✓ Always keep a paper trail of your work and where possible, have customers sign contracts particularly when you're given a deposit for goods in advance.

The key to making it in a crab culture is to let your entrepreneurial actions speak louder than your words or business plans and "cover your back" with a paper trail.

3 - THE PASSIVE SERVICE CULTURE

In a passive service culture, people work to pay bills and do not pursue dream jobs or dream businesses. They passively accept working as human fuel for the dreams of others and do not have a culture of innovation and pursuit of uncommon vision. In this culture, immigrants and foreign nationals who have a dream or commonwealth culture would own most of the significant businesses in the nation. Without them, the nation would not have a thriving business community that creates employment for the citizens and tax revenue for the government.

Let's now examine the features of this culture:

✓ Parents do not encourage their children to dream based on their innate gifts, but rather command them to study to get a job that they can use to pay bills.

✓ In this culture people do not honor their innate gifts and deploy them strategically in the workforce. They tend to take the path of least resistance and find employment doing jobs for which they are not innately gifted.

✓ In this culture people are slothful about pursuing the uncommon dreams within themselves. They prefer to take no risk and become the wheels of the dreams of fearless entrepreneurs who they subconsciously think are better than them.

✓ There are two types of service: **passionate service** and **passive service**. In **passionate service**, people add value to others as they passionately serve their developed gifts and talents. In **passive service**, people give the gift of their time and energy in jobs that they have no passion for and innate skills for.

✓ There is zero innovation, creativity and trail blazing leadership in a passive culture. The people are largely commentators, complainers and followers in everything,.

In summary, in a passive culture people do not pursue dream jobs or dream businesses. They take the path of least resistance and become passive fuel for other people's ideas, solutions and dreams.

4 - A DREAM CULTURE

America is the land of the dream culture. According to Forbes magazine, it currently is the home of the richest man in the world in 2014– Bill Gates. Bill Gates and his company Microsoft personify the dream culture. *The dream culture is about mutual benefit. It is about using your dream to help others fulfill their dreams and they using their dreams to help you fulfill yours and both of you sharing the spoils.* Creating an organization like Microsoft takes more than just one super leader. It takes an army of outstanding men and women who are giving their best to achieve this and Bill Gates has certainly rewarded them. He has rewarded his geniuses with stock just as they rewarded him with their hard work and creativity and they wound up very rich for it. Over ten thousand Microsoft employees have become millionaires through the company's exploits over the past thirty years.

A rich crab entrepreneur would go into a fit if he realizes that his employees are becoming rich through his business. All he wants to do is to give them the minimum to keep them coming back for more. A rich, dream culture entrepreneur finds his joy in seeing you become rich because you're helping him to win and are also winning in the process.

Let's examine the features of this culture in more details:

✓ The dream culture is a win-win culture. There are different human equations in business. There is the "*I win and you lose*" equation which represents a crab culture. There is the "*I lose and you lose*," which is also indicative of the crab culture. There is the "*you win and I lose*," which is the passive service culture. And lastly, there is the "*I win and you win*," which is the dream culture.

✓ People within the dream culture are gift, talent and aptitude inspectors. They search for talent regardless of the package that's carrying it. Once they find it, they build a win-win business around it and the sky is the limit. They even have recruitment consultants called Head Hunters that search for talent.

  ~ In the crab culture they fire bullets at your talent.
  ~ In the passive service culture you hide your talent because of slothfulness.
  ~ In the dream culture, your talent is searched for and rewarded.
  ~ In the commonwealth culture, talent is enthroned.

✓ People within the dream culture celebrate high achievers

✓ People within the dream culture turn into celebrities: people who failed their way into outstanding success. They love a comeback story.

✓ People within that culture study achievers and emulate them.

  ~ In the crab culture they shoot at achievers.
  ~ In the passive service culture, achievers are treated as superior beings.
  ~ In the dream culture, people seek to benefit and learn from achievers.
  ~ In a commonwealth culture, they create enduring platforms for high achievers.

✓ In a dream culture passive service is unrewarded and excellence is rewarded.

In summary, in the dream culture, he who dares the most based on potential achieves wins the most, while making many others win as well.

5 - THE COMMONWEALTH CULTURE

The Commonwealth culture has all the strength and benefits of the dream culture with the added bonus of social responsibility. In a dream culture, the entrepreneur focuses on wining and helping other hardworking people win. In a commonwealth culture, the entrepreneur seeks to do that and create wealth for the community he or she is part of at the same time. They have this philosophy that says, "My wealth is to be used to create commonwealth for all within my community and I am prepared to sacrifice some of it to make that happen." On the other hand, those who are not that successful also have a philosophy that says, "I will sacrifice to keep the entrepreneur successful because I know he will share his wealth with me."

One of my friends in England came from a family that took five brothers out from poverty and made them millionaires in less than forty years. This is their story.

From Poverty to a Family of Millionaires

While in the nation of India, the father of my friend Surag was part of the family of five that was very poor. They had five brothers. They decided to bring all their savings together to send my friend's father to London, England so he could sell cigarettes in the street. The proceeds were to be used to bring the next brother in line to London. When my friend's father got to London, he followed the same plan and within eighteen months the next brother was able to join them. He also was given cigarettes to sell and the same followed for the other brothers. Eventually all five brothers were in England. They kept selling cigarettes in the streets until they could afford to buy a house on a mortgage. Everyone lived in the same house including the new wife of the eldest brother. The next step for them was to open a cash and carry shop where all the brothers worked for stipends. The proceeds of the shop soon became enough to pay off the mortgage and the eldest brother got the house for himself and his wife while the other four brothers moved into the new house. The same pattern was followed until each brother had his own home. By this time of course, the business was booming and eventually they started reaping the profits. Needless to say, all five of them became millionaires.

This is a commonwealth system that is found in certain communities like the Jews, immigrant Indians, and other groups around the world. It is the fastest method of creating generational wealth. The dream culture creates many millionaires however; the commonwealth culture creates generational family wealth and causes small nations like Israel and other immigrant communities to punch in a class much higher than their population weight.

In summary, the commonwealth system creates family generational wealth. The philosophy of using equity financing plus sacrifice with community responsibility creates more wealthy families than any other system.

HYBRID CULTURES

There are many nations that have hybrid cultures. From my research, the culture of the largest population group tends to be the dominant culture. However, there are nations in which other ethnic groups and immigrant populations possess completely different entrepreneurial cultures.

I was born in Gatshead, England, grew up in Sierra Leone and moved back to the United Kingdom when I was twenty years old. I have also traveled extensively and lived for short periods of time in the USA, Canada, St. Lucia and Barbados. I would like to briefly share my findings on the cultures of some of the nations I have lived in:

The United Kingdom

The UK has a dominant dream culture with certain small immigrant population groups having a commonwealth culture.

The United States of America

The USA has a super dream dominant culture with certain small population groups having systemic poverty, passive service and commonwealth cultures.

The Caribbean

Within the Caribbean where I have travelled extensively, there are many nations that have a dominant culture that is part crab and part passive service with a mixture of European diaspora communities having a dream culture and some Indian, Chinese and Middle Eastern communities having a commonwealth culture.

Sierra Leone

In Sierra Leone, I was part of a tribe called the Krio's (Creole). It was made up mostly of intellectuals and had a dream culture with the dominant national culture being a hybrid of passive service and systemic poverty. Immigrant groups like the Lebanese and Indians had a commonwealth culture.

Every Dominant Culture has Exceptions

There will always be people groups who contradict cultural norms in non-entrepreneurial cultural profiles due to many reasons:

1. National and community leaders working to incrementally transform the culture into an idea-based culture and economy.

2. Vision-driven individuals who seek to rise above the mentalities that have kept their family and community in mediocrity.

3. People who have adopted the philosophy of a favorable entrepreneurial culture where they used to live and study.

Also beware that there are people who grew up in dream and commonwealth cultures and because of their choices turn out to be crabs, slothful and passive.

In summary, try to understand the cultural environment in which you are conducting business. Do not paint everybody with the paintbrush of your mental opinions but instead, seek to deal with each individual as they are and not as you may presuppose them to be

STOP AND REFLECT

What is the dominant culture of the nation that you are seeking to do business in and what are the reasons for your conclusion?

_____

_____

_____

_____

_____

_____

_____

Are there any sub-cultures among the other ethnic groups within your nation and what are they?

_____

_____

_____

_____

_____

_____

_____

Entrepreneurial Leadership

5~
Understanding Entrepreneurial Leadership

Entrepreneurial leadership creates influence through the income stream it produces, by selling products that meet the needs of people.

Leadership is using influence to work with and through people to fulfill a vision. People contain skills, abilities, passion and relationships. Leaders have ideas on how the future should be and utilize influence to activate the skills, abilities, passion and relationships of people to take their ideas from concept to reality.

Leadership in its purest form is the application of influence to fulfill a vision. Leadership is needed when a vision requires the participation of more than one person for its fulfillment. Due to the fact that every significant vision on the planet will require the participation of more than one person, leadership is required to bring significant visions from concept to reality.

Vision is the birthplace of reality. It is the fountain that produces the need for leadership. It is a clear mental portrait of a preferred future. It is a picture of what the future looks like if you maximize the potential of a person, people, situation or product. Entrepreneurs are forced to use influence to organize people, money and materials in a structured and systematic way to achieve their predetermined goals. This organizing is called organizational leadership.

If the entrepreneur has a vision and a product that is greater than his ability to organize people, money, and materials to maximize opportunities, he will never fulfill his entrepreneurial potential and in some cases might fail totally.

I have discovered that the greatness of an organization will never emerge until the greatness of its leaders emerges first. As an entrepreneur, if your leadership ability is low, your business development will be kept in check. In other words, *the ceiling of your business is your leadership ability.* In leading an entrepreneurial organization there are certain leadership competences that must be a part of you to maximize your business potential.
They are:

1.   Product Development Competence
2.   Vision Casting Competence
3.   Path-finding Competence
4.   Creating your Dream Team Competence
5.   Organization Alignment Competence
6.   Staff Empowerment Competence
7.   Self Leadership and Modeling Competence

6~

Entrepreneurial Leadership Competences

The skill of the captain of the ship will always affect the quality of the journey in treacherous waters.

You are the captain of the ship of your business. Your staff is your team and your destination represents your business goals. The business environment you operate in provides the waters that your business must sail through. The precious cargo the ship carries is your product. Much can be learnt about leadership from studying the art and science of captaining a ship. This is because the word leadership is made from the words: leader and ship.

Personal success does not automatically translate into leadership success. Success is the progressive realization of predetermined goals. It is about setting a goal to move from point A to point B and you personally getting there. Leadership is different. It is not about you moving from point A to point B; it's about moving a group of people with different gifts, talents, personalities and issues from point A to point B, C and D successfully without losing your mind.

Let us now examine the seven competences of entrepreneurial leadership using the backdrop of successfully captaining a ship:

1. PRODUCT DEVELOPMENT

Selecting the goods and services that the entrepreneurial organization will find markets for and promoting, selling and delivering it to the customer is foundational in every enterprise. This task never ends as product development involves product improvement, product replacement and new product creations to meet market trends. The story of Blackberry, one of the greatest products in recent years, illustrates this point:

BlackBerry: From First Place to Last Place

In 2003 Canadian based Research In Motion (RIM), a little-known maker of pagers, launches the Blackberry smart phone. It was named such because its physical keyboard resembles the small drupelets of the blackberry fruit. It quickly captivated people who wanted email as well as a phone on a mobile device and companies and governments favored its robust secure network. In that year, RIM shares quadrupled to nearly fifteen dollars.

Its rise continued and by October 2007, Blackberry had more than ten million subscribers. It was only a few months after that Apple launched its iPhone and Google joined major wireless carriers and handset makers HTC and Samsung in announcing Android: an open source operating system for smartphones. At this point Blackberry was still the leading brand and had the resources to respond to the changes that were coming in the marketplace.

However, during this period, there were certain key persons within RIM who were convinced that the keypad on the Blackberry would beat the smartphone concept. Now on the other side, was the strategic maneuver by Google in creating the open source operating system for smartphones, which allowed developers to create applications for Android devices. Nevertheless, Blackberry's momentum continued as it would take a while for such a bad strategic decision to affect such a huge billion-dollar business but it was coming.

In June 2008, RIM's shares hit an all time high of 144.56 before the global stock market crashed. February 2009 saw RIM's subscribers top 50 million and the company announced an expansion with thousands of new jobs. However, things were about to change. Blackberry still had an opportunity to respond with a new phone with new features but decided to keep the same model with a few variations. In April 2010, Apple launched the iPad tablet. RIM was then caught flatfooted and responded a year later with the Playbook Tablet, which fell flat. By this time, Apple's iPhone was rising and users were opting for the smartphone model, rather than the keypad model. In July 2011, the inevitable happened and the number of iPhone users surpassed those of Blackberry in the US markets. Shares began to fall and the company announces that two thousand jobs will be cut. The worst was about to follow as Blackberry was now playing catch up in the innovative mobile smartphone race. In 2011, Blackberry users in Europe, the middle East, Africa, India and South America were hit by a service outage which lasted several days. As a result, shares sank below 25 dollars.

The next month, worst news followed: more than half the Smartphones sold worldwide in the third quarter were Android-powered, some 60.5 million units, and Blackberry loses more market share selling only 12.7 million units. The staff cuts and internal turmoil in the company began to take effect and Blackberry users encounter more service problems.

In January 2012, with RIM's share price now below 15 dollars, the company founders Jim Balsillie and Mike Lazaridis resigned as Co.CEO's. Thorsten Heins took over and within two months he releases quarterly earnings showing a loss. In May 2012, RIM hired JPMorgan securities and RBC Capital markets to study its strategic options. They warned of another quarterly loss, cut five thousand jobs and announced that their new platform would be delayed. Shares were now below 10 dollars. In January 2013, RIM launches its new Apple and Android competing platform Blackberry 10. The company changes its name from RIM to Blackberry and recruits singer Alicia Keys as its creative director. The strategy is too little too late and in June 28, 2013, Blackberry posted an unexpected loss of 84 million, sending shares plummeting to the ground. Shipments of the new Z10 and Q10 phones were disappointing. Only 2.7 million were sold in the past quarter. By August 12th of that same year, Blackberry announced that they were studying "strategic alternatives," including the possibility of selling off the firm. By September the company announces that it's cutting 40% of the workforce with a looming loss of 1 billion dollars, all because of its weak response to a drastic shift in market conditions. In September 23, 2013, Blackberry agrees to a 4.7 billion buyout by a consortium of investors who planned to take the smartphone maker private.

The story of Blackberry illustrates the power of product development. They went from a small pager maker company to a global entity with global influence. However, they got seduced and deceived into complacency by their meteoric success.

2. VISION CASTING

Leaders shape the future with ideas that have become fully developed visions. These visions are the shape of the future that guide the entrepreneurial leader's day-to-day actions. *Authentic vision is the ability to see a future that belongs to you and take steps every day to align yourself to the manifestation of it.* True vision is not a pipe dream. It is the pictures of what the future can be if you develop what you already have access to. It is the picture of the tomato fruit on a packet of tomato seeds. The vision of the fruit of a venture never looks like the seed of the venture. Just like the tomato fruit looks very different from the tomato seed, so will your fully developed business look very different from your startup business. Vision casting is the skill of compellingly communicating your vision to those whose participation in its fulfillment is critical to its success.

One of the common mistakes that immature visionaries make, is they focus on the features of the vision. Mature visionaries do not do that. They focus on the problem the vision is designed to solve. They focus on the benefits of the vision to the marketplace and customers and they do this because they understand that business is about solving problems for people at a profit.

Your vision will have many features, however, you must learn how to communicate it to your circle of success relationships.

These are:

1. Investors – They are more focused on the profits your business can generate for them and your ability to deliver and be a safe pair of hands. When you share a vision to investors, focus on the potential return on investments rather than all the features of the product and venture.

2. Partners – They are interested in the process, products, promotion, marketing and the systems that would guarantee success. They want to know where they fit in your vision and whether you can be trusted with their investment of time, treasure and talent.

3. Staff – They want to know that your vision can add value to them financially and in some cases, give them a dream job. They will quickly figure out your philosophy, that is whether you care only about their output or about them as well.

4. Customers – They are not interested in your profit margins, systems, and processes or staff development. What they are interested in is how your product can solve a problem for them at a price they can afford.

3. PATH-FINDING

True leaders see beyond where the organization is and are constantly plotting out the best course to take to achieve the mission of the organization. Path-finding involves both strategic planning and tactical maneuvers. Strategy is a series of sequential synchronize steps to take you from your current reality to your desired future. Good strategic planning always begins with a brutally honest definition of current reality. It then accurately discerns the possibility of the future and creates a path to get there using first, second and third order affect. A great example of the power of strategic planning can be seen in the rise and sustained success of Japanese companies like Sony, Toyota, Panasonic who have fifty to hundred years strategic plans.

Tactical intelligence on the other hand, is the ability to quickly perceive a situation, evaluate multiple scenarios and take the necessary actions to get the desired results. Great companies follow a well thought-out strategic plan, and in the heat of fast changing situations, make wise tactical decisions that cause them to win. The task of navigational leadership involves both tactics and strategy.

4. CREATING YOUR DREAM TEAM

The leadership of an organization will determine its rise or fall. The vision of an organization determines its focus and effectiveness. The structure of an organization will determine its behavior. The people within the organization determine its potential.

People are the potentially appreciating assets within organizations. Attracting the right people to your business and putting them in the right place on the bus is indispensable. The type of people you have in your organization matters. As the CEO of your business, you are the chief cultural officer by default and it's in your best interest to create a culture that attracts, maintains and rewards excellence.

5. ORGANIZATIONAL ALIGNMENT

Management is the optimum stewardship of existing resources to meet predetermined objectives. Entrepreneurial leaders, though rich with human resources, material resources, financial assets and brand loyalty, can fail if they do not align these four elements in a structured and strategic way to achieve predetermined objectives. Many times successful companies lose their market leadership because they fail to realign their organization to` a changing dynamic in the economy and marketplace. This was the case for Blockbuster, RIM and many others.

6. MODELING

The key question I ask entrepreneurial leaders on the subject of modeling and self-leadership is this: if the members of your team had your passion, integrity and competence will the company succeed or fail? Self-leadership is the ability to master yourself so that you bring the best out of yourself. It is the opposite of self-sabotage.

Dennis Kozski: The Penalty of Poor Self-Leadership Integrity

The story of Tyco illustrates this: Tyco's CEO Dennis Kozski was a celebrity CEO. His company and his exploits were touted as a model of business leadership for a season However, Dennis Kozski and his CFO Mark Swartz were found guilty of twenty counts of grand larceny and conspiracy, falsifying business records and violating general business law. They were accused of taking bonuses worth more than a 120 million without the approval of Tyco directors, abusing an employee loan program, and misrepresenting the company's financial condition to investors to boost the stock price while selling 575 million in stock.

Dennis Kozski was an immensely talented man who spoke at CEO leadership conferences, but he let himself down by not leading himself positively. Instead, he lead himself into prison. Success that is not built on the platform of self-leadership would eventually come crashing down. The stories of Enron and Arthur Anderson illustrate this.

STOP AND REFLECT

On a scale of 1 to 10 assess your current level of strength in these leadership competences.

1. Product Development

1	2	3	4	5	6	7	8	9	10

2. Vision Casting

1	2	3	4	5	6	7	8	9	10

3.Path-finding

1	2	3	4	5	6	7	8	9	10

4.   Creating Your Dream Team

1	2	3	4	5	6	7	8	9	10

5.   Organizational Alignment

1	2	3	4	5	6	7	8	9	10

6.   Modeling

1	2	3	4	5	6	7	8	9	10

YOU
CAN
DO
IT

7~

A Formula For Entrepreneurial Success

A formula is a concise way of expressing information symbolically as in a mathematical or chemical formula

MY SUCCESS FORMULA IS AS FOLLOWS:

Entrepreneurial success is guaranteed when you are inspired by an authentic vision guided by good strategy, propelled by wise product development, anchored by personal growth, distinguished by excellence, focused on customer service and responsive to market trends.

1 - Inspired By Authentic Vision

Authentic vision is a clear mental portrait of a future and potential you can possess. It is the source of sustained inspiration. Potential it is what you can be, do and have if you keep developing yourself. This vision is a portrait of the greatest version of your business. When that inspires you, your foundation is solid. Your foundation is not solid when your inspiration and motivation to start a business is what your competition, friends or enemies are doing. The energy produced by that is not sustainable and can become destructive.

2 - Guided By Strategy

Once your vision has been defined, time must be taken to think ahead and plan your steps, as business is strategy intensive. This is due to the fact that your market is constantly evolving and you must anticipate where the market is going to create products that will meet the needs of the market. Taking the time to create a plan that contains a clear definition of your current reality with sequential synchronized steps to take you from that reality to the realization of your vision is indispensable. An immature entrepreneur is guided by the options that scream the loudest, however, mature prudent entrepreneurs are guided by their predetermined, well thought-out strategic objectives.

3 - Propelled By Product Development Wisdom

The propeller that drives your business venture must be getting the right product at the right time to the right market at a price that market can afford. It also involves continually improving existing products and securing the long-term viability of the business venture through new product development, mergers and acquisitions, if required.

4 - Anchored By Personal Growth

The summit and ceiling of a company, department or team is the leadership ability of the person in charge. When that person's ability is high and growing, their future is bright but when it's low, mediocrity, losses and failure are around the corner. Investing in your personal growth as an entrepreneurial leader is the greatest anchor that your business can have, because as you grow, the business grows.

5 - Distinguished By Excellence

Excellence is representing the product of your person, services and goods to the best of your current ability. Excellence is relative as one person's excellence could be another person's minimum output. It is the extra touch that makes a difference and gives you, your products and your company the extra shine. Excellence is very personal and focuses on individuals, teams and organizations putting their best foot forward with the resources they currently have and not what they don't have. John Mason, in his book, An Enemy Called Average states that, *taking the path of least resistance is what makes men and rivers crooked*. Excellence is not the path of least resistance. It is the best from you.

6 - Focused On Customer Service And Responsive To Market Trends

Focus is concentrating on the priorities that are required to acquire what you desire. Mike Murdock, an esteemed success teacher often says, *the number one reason why men fail, is broken focus.* All prudent entrepreneurs know that the needs and desires of the customer is king. Attempting to impose your desires and your perspectives on customers is not a guaranteed plan for success. However, developing products and providing service that meet their evolving needs is critical to your longevity in business.

About The Author

Andre Thomas is a Thought Leader, Author, Leadership Coach and Executive Strategy Consultant. He has worked as a Consultant for numerous organizations including: Government Agencies, Business Organizations and Social Organizations

He has conducted numerous seminars for the Private-sector, the United Nations (UN), Government and Non-governmental Agencies.

Thought Leader and Author

Andre Thomas is a Strategic Thinker on the subject of Leadership for The Transformation of Nations and a prolific author on the subject of leadership. His books include:

1.   The Organizational Visionary *(The Dynamics of Organizational Leadership)*
2.   The Gift of Political Leadership

3. 12 Spheres of Leadership *(The 12 Types of Leaders That Shape The Destinies Of Nations)*
4. Unlock Your Greatness *(A Young Leaders' Handbook)*
5. Discovering Me
6. Uncommon Men and Distinguished Women
7. Coaching People into the 12 Spheres of Leadership
8. Seven Principles of Commonwealth Leadership
9. Discovering your Leadership Assignment
10. Preparing for your Leadership Assignment
11. Executing your Leadership Assignment
12. I Am A Leader *(Inspiring Greatness in Kids)*
13. The Entrepreneurial Visionary *(The Dynamics of Entrepreneurial Leadership)*
14. From Brokenness to Wholeness *(Overcoming the Storms and LifeQuakes of Life)*

Leadership Coach

Andre Thomas is a Dynamic Leadership Coach that motivates and teaches the concepts and mechanics of leadership in a way that all ages and levels of society can understand. His seminars have included participants from Private, Social, Governmental and Non-Governmental Sectors.

Executive Strategy and Governance Consultant

Andre Thomas is a Gifted Executive Strategy Consultant with a wealth of experience in creating strategic solutions for leaders and organizational development solutions for organizations.

He is the founder and president of The Ideas and Solutions Group::A group of organizations that work through strategic partnerships, events, coaching, media, resources and consulting to create a leadership wisdom culture in organizations and nations that takes ideas and solutions from concept to reality.

Websites

www.ideasandsolutions.org

The Ideas And Solutions Group

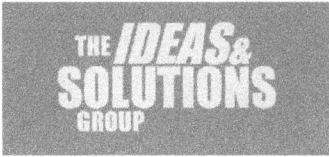

Purpose

To equip a critical mass of leaders in nations to bring ideas and solutions from concept to reality through the principles and process of transformational leadership and economic dignity

Vision

To see transformation occur in nations and their economies as leaders emerge to bring ideas and solutions from concept to reality.

Philosophy

1. The problems of a generation will never be greater than the ideas and solutions within people born into that generation

2. These ideas and solutions are within people in the form of an uncommon vision

3. Leadership wisdom is applying principles and taking steps to take ideas and solutions from concept to reality

4. Except the leadership wisdom operating the visionary matches the scope of the vision, the uncommon vision within them will not be fulfilled

Other Books By Greatness Publishing

GREATNESS
PUBLISHING

Nina D Thomas

1.   Woman, Get Off that Bus

Andre Thomas

1.   The Organizational Visionary   *(The Dynamics of Organizational Leadership)*
2.   The Gift of Political Leadership
3.   12 Spheres of Leadership *(The 12 Types of Leaders That Shape The Destinies Of Nations)*
4.   Unlock Your Greatness *(A Young Leaders' Handbook)*
5.   Discovering Me
6.   Uncommon Men and Distinguished Women

7. Coaching People into the 12 Spheres of Leadership
8. Seven Principles of Commonwealth Leadership
9. Discovering your Leadership Assignment
10. Preparing for your Leadership Assignment
11. Executing your Leadership Assignment
12. I Am a Leader *(Inspiring Greatness in Kids)*
13. From Brokenness to Wholeness *(Overcoming the Storms and LifeQuakes of Life)*

To make bulk purchases email us at:

COO@IDEASANDSOLUTIONS.ORG

www.ingramcontent.com/pod-product-compliance
Lightning Source LLC
Chambersburg PA
CBHW060644210326
41520CB00010B/1739